HEROES OF HISTORY

I0794500

INNOVATORS

Written by Anita Ganeri
Illustrated by Joe Todd Stanton

PowerKiDS press

Published in 2026 by The Rosen Publishing Group, Inc.
2544 Clinton Street, Buffalo, NY 14224

Created by:
Author: Anita Ganeri
Additional text: Nicola Barber
Illustrator: Joe Todd Stanton
Additional Illustrations: Katie Abey
Editorial: Hannah Wilson, Lydia Halliday
Senior Designer: Krina Patel
Designer: Natasha Rees
Index: Vanessa Bird

Cataloging-in-Publication Data

Names: Ganeri, Anita, 1961, author. | Todd-Stanton, Joe, illustrator.

Title: Innovators / by Anita Ganeri, illustrated by Joe Todd-Stanton.

Description: Buffalo, NY : PowerKids Press, 2026. | Series: Heroes of history | Includes glossary and index.

Identifiers: ISBN 9781499454871 (pbk.) | ISBN 9781499454888 (library bound) | ISBN 9781499454895 (ebook)

Subjects: LCSH: Scientists--Biography--Juvenile literature. | Inventors--Biography--Juvenile literature. | Technological innovations--Juvenile literature.

Classification: LCC Q141.G364 2026 | DDC 509.2’2--dc23

Manufactured in the United States of America

CPSIA Compliance Information: Batch #CSPK26. For further information contact Rosen Publishing at 1-800-237-9932.

CONTENTS

INTRODUCTION

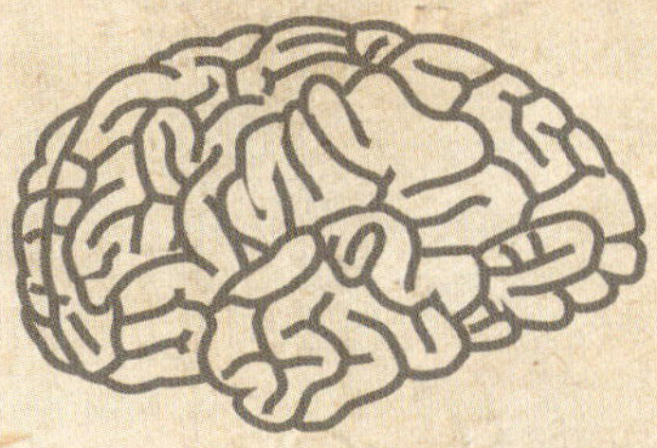

History is packed with heroes and heroines who left a lasting legacy behind. Some were larger-than-life characters, born leaders who inspired their followers. Others worked away quietly, shunning the limelight. They earned their fame in different ways - through hard work, determination and, sometimes, sheer luck.

INNOVATORS

Discovering something new is exciting at the best of times but especially so if the innovation (invention or discovery) has a major impact on the course of history. Some amazing discoveries like these were made accidentally. Others were the result of years of failure, success and lots of hard work.

Aristotle

Leonardo da Vinci

The incredible innovators behind these discoveries, which still influence the way people think and view the world, are not only heroes of history but also household names.

In this chapter, you can read about an Ancient Greek philosopher; an artist, inventor, and all-round genius from Italy; a scientist who worked out how we all got here; and a chemist who revolutionized healthcare.

Marie Curie

Charles Darwin

ARISTOTLE

Father of Philosophy

One of the greatest philosophers who has ever lived, Aristotle's work covered a huge range of subjects, from poetry and politics to science and natural history. His ideas influenced Western ways of thinking for almost 2,000 years after his death and are still studied today.

Early days

Aristotle was born in 384 BCE in Stagira, a small town on the coast of northern Greece. His father, Nicomachus, was royal doctor to King Amyntas II of Macedonia. Little is known about Aristotle's childhood, but it seems likely that, because of his father's work, he spent time at the Macedonian court. Nicomachus died when Aristotle was just a young boy (Aristotle's mother had also died), and Aristotle's brother-in-law, Proxenus, became his guardian.

The Academy

When Aristotle turned 18, Proxenus sent him to Athens to continue his education. At that time, Athens was considered to be the academic center of the world. Aristotle entered the Academy, a school set up by the philosopher Plato. He was to stay there for the next 20 years, first as a brilliant student and later as a teacher. Subjects were not taught in set classes. Instead, students challenged each other with questions and took part in lively debates.

When Plato died in 347 BCE, it was expected that Aristotle would take over as director of the Academy, but he was not offered the post. This may have been because he had disagreed with some of Plato's philosophical ideas. Plato's nephew was appointed director instead. Bitterly disappointed, Aristotle left Athens. He headed to Asia Minor (modern day Turkey) to the court of his friend King Hermias.

ARISTOTLE'S PHILOSOPHY DIARY

About 345 BCE
Lesbos, Greece

Since I left Athens, I've been busier than ever. For a start, I got married — to Hermias' niece, Pythias. I've also been spending lots of time here on the island of Lesbos, with my friend and fellow philosopher Theophrastus. He's been studying plants, and I've been studying animals, especially sea creatures. Fascinating things. I've been dissecting them to find out more (no one else is doing this, but I reckon it'll catch on).

343 BCE
Pella, Macedonia

I'm back in Macedonia. Well, it was a job offer I couldn't refuse. King Philip II wanted me to start tutoring his son, Alexander. He's only 13, but he's very smart and destined for great things, I'll bet. I've already given him some tips on leadership. Anyway, it's all going well, so far, and the king's been very generous.

335 BCE
Athens, Greece

Alexander is king now and is busy conquering the world, including Athens, so it was safe for me to head back to the city. I've started my own school — the Lyceum — and I'm rushed off my feet, teaching, researching and writing. I walk around the grounds while I'm teaching so the students have to follow me — that keeps them on their toes.

About 330 BCE
The Lyceum, Athens

A great day! We opened our new library and already there are thousands of scrolls on the shelves. Some of them are my own work, but there are also works by other philosophers, including Theophrastus, and some of the students' own research. I want it to become the greatest library in the world.

323 BCE
Athens, Greece

Bad news — Alexander has died. They think he had a fever, but no one's really sure. Here in Athens, there's been a lot of anti-Macedonian feeling and it's not a very comfortable place to be. I've even been accused of not holding the gods in honor. It's a trumped-up charge, of course, but if I stay here, I'll be arrested. I've decided to flee to Chalcis (on the island of Euboea). My mother's family owns some land there so, hopefully, I'll be safe.

MIND-BLOWING PHILOSOPHERS

Like Aristotle, all of the teachers and philosophers on these pages have influenced the way other people have thought, and their ideas continue to be important today.

Statue of Aristotle in Stagira, Greece

Influential ideas

In 322 BCE, Aristotle fled to Chalcis to escape arrest and possible execution in Athens. He died later that same year. His writings were rediscovered and widely read during the Middle Ages. Aristotle's philosophy came to form the basis for Western thought for many centuries.

Chinese philosopher Confucius

Confucius

As a young man, Confucius studied the Six Arts — ritual, music, archery, chariot-driving, calligraphy, and mathematics. These were considered essential in China. Later, Confucius taught the need to lead by example and with compassion.

René Descartes, 1596–1650

René Descartes

Descartes, a French philosopher, scientist, and mathematician now known as the "Father of Modern Philosophy," refused to accept the authority of earlier philosophers such as Aristotle. He questioned everything, and his most famous saying was: "I think, therefore I exist."

Timeline of philosophers

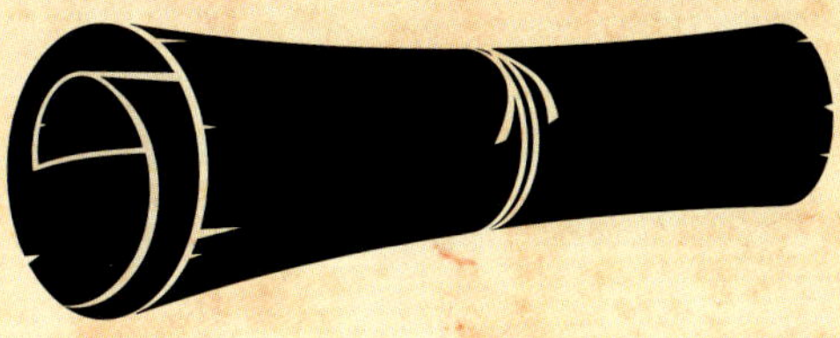

479 BCE
Confucius

Chinese teacher, whose philosophy becomes widespread in China and beyond, dies.

335 BCE
Aristotle

Greek philosopher begins writing some of the most influential works in Western thought.

*c.*1012 CE
Avicenna

Persian philosopher and scientist begins writing *The Canon of Medicine*. The text remains in use for centuries.

1641
René Descartes

French philosopher, scientist, and mathematician publishes *Meditations on First Philosophy*, which is still studied today.

1867
Karl Marx

German philosopher and revolutionary thinker publishes the first volume of *Das Kapital*, written with Friedrich Engels.

Leonardo da Vinci

All-round Genius

Leonardo da Vinci may be best known as the artist who created the mysterious *Mona Lisa*, one of the most famous paintings of all time. But he was also a talented sculptor, engineer, scientist, inventor, writer, and architect — the list goes on and on.

Early life

Leonardo was born on April 15, 1452, in Vinci, a town near Florence, Italy. His father, Piero, was a wealthy lawyer and his mother, Caterina, was a poor farm worker. The two were not married and Leonardo did not have a family name. His surname "da Vinci," simply means "from Vinci."

For the first few years, Leonardo lived with his mother in the small village of Anchiano. Then, he went to live with his father, step-mother, and grandparents back in Vinci. Little is known about his childhood. He probably did not go to school, but learned some Latin, math, and geometry. He must also have shown some promise as an artist.

Budding artist

Leonardo's father was well respected in Florence society. When Leonardo was 14 years old, his father found him a place as an apprentice of the painter and sculptor Andrea del Verrochio, in Florence. Verrochio's workshop was said to be the finest in Florence, and many other famous painters worked there. For the next six years, Leonardo learned a wide range of skills, including drawing, sculpting, carpentry, and metalwork. The workshop also produced paintings, many of which were done by Leonardo and the other trainees. Leonardo learned fast. By the time he was 20 years old, he was ready to branch out on his own.

LEONARDO'S ARTISTIC DIARY

Sometime in 1472
Florence, Italy

Brilliant news! I've passed my apprenticeship and I'm a master painter. I've joined the Guild of St. Luke and even have my own workshop (thanks, Dad). But I've still been working with Verrochio on *The Baptism of Christ*. He let me paint the angel holding Jesus' robe and it's turned out well, I reckon. In fact, Verrochio says I've done such a great job that he's giving up painting for good.

Sometime in 1497
Milan, Italy

It's finished. I can't believe it. After two years of painting, *The Last Supper* is done. I just hope the Duke of Milan (he commissioned it) is pleased. It has been a long, hard project. Some days, I painted from dawn to dusk without stopping to eat. But then, it does cover the whole wall of the convent dining hall, so I always knew it would be a long job.

Sometime in 1502
Cesena, Italy
I'm in Cesena, working for Cesare Borgia, Duke of Valentinois. To get the job, I had to draw a map of the town of Imola. The Duke was so impressed that he took me on as his chief engineer. He's kept me busy drawing more maps and designing a dam.

Sometime in 1504
Florence, Italy

Back in Florence, a merchant, Francesco del Giocondo, asked me to paint a portrait of his wife, Lisa. I've given her a mysterious smile and added a shadowy feel. The painting — I've called it *Mona Lisa* — is for their new home. It'll take me a few more years to finish, and by then I might not want to part with it at all.

Sometime around 1505
Florence, Italy
I've been looking at how birds fly and am designing a flying machine! I've got a few ideas. The best is the ornithopter, a machine with flapping wings where the pilot lies flat on a board. I can't wait to start building and get this beauty off the ground.

INVENTIVE GENIUSES

Leonardo da Vinci is best remembered for the *Mona Lisa* (which he never did deliver to the merchant). But like all the geniuses here, his curiosity led him towards other ideas and subjects.

Leonardo da Vinci, who died in 1519

Last years

Leonardo returned to Milan and studied anatomy, even cutting up corpses. In 1516, he went to France to work for King Francis I, spending his last years living near the king's summer palace at Amboise. As well as famous paintings, Leonardo left behind thousands of notes and drawings.

Archimedes

Archimedes devised mathematical theories still used today. Also an inventor, he designed the Archimedes screw, a machine to raise water from a lower to a higher level. In 214 BCE, he invented a new catapult to repel invaders.

Archimedes, born in Syracuse c.287 BCE

A waxwork figure of Albert Einstein

Albert Einstein

In 1905, German-born physicist Albert Einstein published four scientific papers that changed modern physics. Soon famous, he won the Nobel Prize for Physics in 1921. Later, Einstein warned the U.S. President Franklin Delano Roosevelt that the Nazis were developing a nuclear bomb.

Timeline of great thinkers

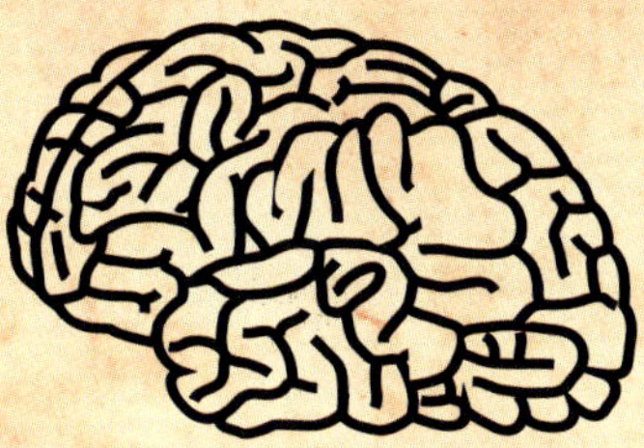

*c.*212 BCE

Archimedes

Greek mathematician, astronomer, inventor, and engineer dies after the siege of Syracuse in Sicily.

*c.*1504 CE

Leonardo da Vinci

Italian Renaissance artist paints his most famous work, *Mona Lisa.*

1687

Isaac Newton

English scientist and mathematician, a key figure in the scientific revolution, publishes *Principia,* outlining the laws of motion and gravity.

1774

Johann von Goethe

German poet, novelist, and politician publishes *The Sorrows of Young Werther.* The book makes him a celebrity.

1905

Albert Einstein

German physicist publishes four ground-breaking scientific papers and goes on to develop the theory of relativity.

Charles Darwin

Life Scientist

In 1831, British naturalist Charles Darwin set off on a journey that not only changed his own life, but transformed the way people think about the natural world. He discovered that species change over time to suit their environment.

Early life

Charles Darwin was born on February 12, 1809, in Shrewsbury, England. His father, Robert, was a wealthy doctor, and the family lived in a large house, called The Mount. From a young age, Charles was much more interested in animals and nature than he was in schoolwork. Even so, in 1825, he set off for Edinburgh University to study medicine. But, quickly, he realized he wasn't cut out for it. He found the lectures boring and hated the sight of blood.

Exasperated, Charles' father let him leave Edinburgh and go to Cambridge University to train as a clergyman. Charles soon got bored of that, too. He preferred to spend his time going for long walks in the countryside, collecting beetles — although he did manage to pass his degree. After university, Charles spent the summer in Wales, studying rock formations and trying to decide what to do next.

Voyage of the *Beagle*

When Charles got home, he found a letter waiting for him. It would change his life. It offered him a job as a ship's naturalist on board HMS *Beagle*, which was about to set off on a two-year voyage to chart the coastline of South America. Charles' father was appalled. His son had already dropped out of medicine and now he was thinking about running away to sea. But Charles had his Uncle Jos (Josiah Wedgwood) on his side. Josiah thought it was a brilliant idea, and persuaded Robert to let Charles go.

CHARLES' EVOLUTION DIARY

January 18, 1832
Cape Verde Islands
Dry land at last! I'm so relieved. We set off from Plymouth three weeks ago and I've been seasick ever since. Also, I'm sharing a cabin with Captain Fitzroy and it's a bit of a squeeze. Anyway, things are looking up. I've had a fantastic few days, exploring the islands and collecting samples of rocks, plants, and animals, including a couple of octopuses that keep changing color — how brilliant is that?

April 26, 1832
Botafogo, Brazil
We're here in Brazil and I've moved into a little cottage in Botafogo, near Rio de Janeiro. I've spent every day exploring the rainforest. It's packed with more animals and plants than I've ever seen in my life — it's like heaven on Earth to me. I've seen howler monkeys, sloths, and caimans and, in one day alone, I collected SIXTY-EIGHT species of beetle!

September 25, 1832
Punta Alta, Argentina
What a day! I was wandering along the beach when I noticed something sticking out of the cliff. I set to work with my pickax and soon had a great pile of fossilized bones and teeth. They must have belonged to some big, and I mean GIGANTIC, prehistoric animals. I've also dug out a massive rhino skull and some bones from a giant sloth. The question is, how am I going to get this lot back on board?

August 1834
Valparaiso, Chile
I've been riding and hiking in the Andes Mountains (I got my walking boots sent over from England). There's so much to see. On one mountain slope, I spotted a band of seashell fossils. How on Earth did they get here? Clearly, these mountains must once have been under the sea. I'm going to have to investigate.

October 20, 1835
Galapagos Islands, Ecuador
What an extraordinary place. It's full of amazing animals you don't find anywhere else, but it's the finches that really fascinate me. Each island has its own kind, with a slightly different-shaped beak. They must have started off the same, but gradually evolved different beaks for eating different types of food. That way, there's less competition for food.

SUPER SCIENTISTS

Like Darwin, all of the scientists on these pages spent many years researching and making observations before coming up with their groundbreaking ideas and discoveries.

Statue of Darwin, who died in 1882

Natural selection

Charles Darwin returned to England in 1836 and wrote about his amazing expedition. He realized that the species that adapted to their environment survived, while those that didn't died off. He developed his "theory of natural selection" for 20 years before announcing it in 1858.

Gregor Mendel

From 1856 to 1863, Mendel studied plants and flowers, noting how color, size, and shape were passed down from one generation to another. In the 1900s, scientists realized the importance of Mendel's research into genetics.

Austrian naturalist Gregor Mendel

Alexander Fleming, born in 1881

Alexander Fleming

After a holiday, Scottish scientist Alexander Fleming returned to his laboratory to find a strange mold growing in a dish containing germs. The mold had destroyed the germs around it. He named it penicillin. One of the first antibiotics to be discovered, it has since saved millions of lives.

Timeline of life scientists

1799
Alexander von Humboldt

Prussian geographer and explorer begins his travels in Central and South America, gathering huge amounts of information.

1859
Charles Darwin

British naturalist publishes *On the Origin of Species*, detailing his theory of natural selection.

1863
Louis Pasteur

French chemist invents the process of pasteurization and later, in 1881, develops vaccines against anthrax and, in 1885, rabies.

1866
Gregor Mendel

Founder of the modern science of genetics publishes his findings.

1928
Alexander Fleming

Medical scientist discovers penicillin, one of the first antibiotics.

Marie Curie

Brilliant Mind

As a woman, Marie Curie had to work hard to prove herself, but she became one of the most famous scientists in the world. At the end of the nineteenth century, she discovered a brand-new chemical element — radium. The discovery changed the path of science.

Early life

Marie Sklodowska was born on November 7, 1867 in Warsaw, Poland, the youngest of five children. Both of Marie's parents were teachers. Her mother was the head of the boarding school where the family lived. When Marie was 10 years old, her mother died. Marie was devastated and hid her feelings by burying herself in her books. She read everything she could find — adventure stories, poetry, and her father's science books.

At school, Marie was a brilliant pupil. In 1883, she graduated from high school top of her class with a gold medal for outstanding achievement. Marie and her sister, Bronya, longed to carry on studying, but Warsaw University did not take girls as students. Marie came up with a plan. With their savings, the sisters would send Bronya to Paris, France, to study medicine. Then, when she qualified as a doctor, she would send for Marie.

Paris and Pierre

In 1891, Marie finally left for Paris and the Sorbonne University. She took her studies very seriously and, just two years later, gained a degree in physics. The following year, she earned a degree in mathematics.

At the same time, Marie met Pierre Curie, a lecturer at the School of Physics and Chemistry. The two were married on July 26, 1895. Afterwards, Marie began studying for her Doctor of Science, investigating the mysterious rays given off by the metal uranium.

MARIE'S CHEMISTRY DIARY

December 26, 1898
Paris, France

We've been working away in our laboratory (a leaky shed), analyzing lumps of pitchblende (a type of rock). We knew it contained uranium, but the rays were so strong, we reckoned there must be something else. Back in July, we discovered a new chemical element, which we called polonium, after Poland. And today, we've discovered a second — radium. Now we want a sample and for that we'll need tons of pitchblende.

December 1903
Paris, France

What a year it's been. In June, I gained my Doctor of Science so I'm now Dr. Curie! And, a few days ago, we heard the news that we (together with Henri Becquerel) have been awarded the Nobel Prize in Physics. I'm the first woman to win. We're not going to Stockholm for the presentation — we're too busy with our work. But we'll use the money to hire a lab assistant as we've never had one before.

May 1906
Paris, France

I don't know how to write this. My heart is broken. On April 19, Pierre was crossing the road and was killed by a horse-drawn wagon. The university has offered me Pierre's old job, as Professor of Physics, and I've accepted as a tribute to him. I began my first lecture in exactly the same place that Pierre finished his.

December 1911
Stockholm, Sweden

I've been awarded another Nobel Prize, this time in Chemistry. I'm the first person ever to win two, I'm told. This time, I'm going to Stockholm to receive the prize. And I'm going to use any influence I have to persuade the government to support my new Radium Institute where we can carry out research. Then I'm going to have a rest – I'm completely worn out.

August 1914
Paris, France

I'm delighted to say that the Radium Institute is now open on a street that has been newly renamed Rue Pierre-Curie. He would have been so proud. Sadly, we are also at war so I've volunteered for war work. My daughter Irène and I are fitting up vans with mobile X-ray machines so that we can reach wounded soldiers on the battlefield. They've been nicknamed *Petites Curies* ("Little Curies").

AMAZING MINDS

Marie Curie's amazing mind made her the only woman to win Nobel prizes in two different fields (physics and chemistry). Here are other people with brilliant minds.

Polish-French physicist Marie Curie

Leading lady

After the war, Marie continued work at her Radium Institute, unaware that the exposure to radiation was slowly killing her — the dangers were not known at the time. She died in 1934, having laid the foundations for innovations such as nuclear power and some cancer treatments.

Galileo Galilei

When Galileo heard about the invention of the first telescope, he built a more powerful version and took up astronomy. But he was accused of heresy after supporting the theory that the sun (not Earth) is at the universe's center.

Galileo Galilei, 1564-1642

Alan Turing, 1912-1954

Alan Turing

Turing studied maths at Cambridge University. There, he developed the Turing machine — the basis of the modern computer. During World War II, he worked at Bletchley Park, the ultra-secret code-breaking centre. After the war, he continued his work on early computers and artificial intelligence.

Timeline of incredible scientists

1609
Johannes Kepler

German mathematician and astronomer publishes *New Astronomy*, about the motion of planets around the sun.

1638
Galileo Galilei

Italian mathematician, scientist, and astronomer publishes *Discourses Concerning Two New Sciences* while under house arrest.

1898
Marie Curie

Scientist discovers radium while investigating radioactivity with her husband Pierre.

1939
Alan Turing

British mathematician begins code-breaking at Bletchley Park. His work during World War II (1939-1945) helps to save lives and shorten the war.

1988
Stephen Hawking

British physicist and cosmologist, known for his work on black holes and quantum mechanics, publishes *A Brief History of Time*, which becomes a bestseller.

GLOSSARY

apprentice Someone who works for and receives training from an expert in a field.

architect A person who designs buildings and oversees construction.

caligraphy Beautiful or artistic writing.

chemical element A substance that cannot be broken down into simpler substances (such as oxygen, gold, and radium).

comology A branch of science that deals with the nature of the universe.

genetics A branch of biology that deals with inherited traits and variation of species.

radiation Energy emitted in the form of waves or particles.

FOR MORE INFORMATION

Stanley, Joseph. *Marie Curie*. Buffalo, NY: Cavendish Square, 2025.

Walter, Isaacson. *Albert Einstein: The Man, the Genius, and the Theory of Relativity*. Buffalo, NY: Rosen Publishing, 2021.

Charles Darwin's Ideas of Evolution
www.bbc.co.uk/bitesize/articles/zfbjxg8#zvc2h4j

INDEX